Go Away!

Written by Jo Windsor

Rigby

Here is the lizard.
Go away!

lizard

Here is the fish.
Go away!

fish

Here is the porcupine.
Go away!

porcupine

Here is the monkey.
Go away!

monkey

Here is the octopus.
Go away!

octopus

Here is the fish.
Go away!

fish

Index

▬▬ Guide Notes

Title: Go Away!

Stage: Emergent – Magenta

Genre: Nonfiction (Expository)

Approach: Guided Reading

Processes: Thinking Critically, Exploring Language, Processing Information

Written and Visual Focus: Photographs (static images), Index, Labels

Word Count: 36

FORMING THE FOUNDATION

Tell the children that this book is about animals that can frighten other animals.
Talk to them about what is on the front cover. Read the title and the author.
Focus the children's attention on the index and talk about the animals that are
in this book.
"Walk" through the book, focusing on the photographs and talk about the different
animals and how they could frighten another animal.

Read the text together.

THINKING CRITICALLY

(sample questions)

After the reading
- Why do you think some animals would want to frighten another animal?
- What other animals do you know that frighten other animals?

EXPLORING LANGUAGE

(ideas for selection)

Terminology
Title, cover, author, photographs

Vocabulary
Interest words: lizard, fish, porcupine, monkey, octopus
High-frequency words: here, is, the